Wild Bird World

Wild Bird World

Written and Illustrated by

C. B. Colby

Franklin Watts, Inc.
575 Lexington Avenue
New York, N.Y. 10022

Cover drawings show the cedar waxwing (top) and the tufted puffin. For information on these birds see pages 65 and 56.

SBN 531 00698-0

2   3   4   5

Contents

Foreword

After reading about the birds in this book, and looking at the sketches, I hope that you will want to know more about all birds. Almost every backyard, park, highway, or even city street has some sort of birdlife in or on it. Of course, the farther you go from the city the closer you come to more and more interesting species.

Each area of the United States has its own particular abundant species, every state has its official bird, and every bird watcher has his favorite. Our country has its own official bird — the bald eagle (although the wild turkey was almost chosen instead, back in 1782 when the selection was made).

There are many different kinds of birds with many different habits. Birds of prey live on other birds, reptiles, fish, and mammals. There are also songbirds, seabirds, shorebirds, and game birds. Some birds, like the starling, always seem to be increasing in numbers, while others, such as the great auk, the passenger pigeon, the Labrador duck, and the Carolina parakeet, have been largely exterminated by man or man and a combination of other circumstances.

1

Even today, despite the many conservation programs, several species are on the verge of extinction. These include the giant California condor and the ivory-billed woodpecker. Perhaps there are already too few of these birds left, and other species as well, to be saved from extinction.

Birds have many interesting habits and personality traits. There are "good guys" and "bad guys" in every species — delinquents, smart alecks, Pollyannas, and the just plain stupid. The more you watch and study bird habits, the more you will recognize their individual traits. The more you watch them, the more you will find to interest and amuse you.

Studying the habits of birds takes patience, sharp eyes or binoculars, and a few quarts of seeds. A feeding tray in your backyard or on your windowsill will give you hours of entertainment, as well as a ringside look at some handsome performers.

Even after sundown, bird activity continues; some of our most interesting species do their "shopping" after dark. The nighthawks, whippoorwills, owls, and others who hunt by twilight and on into the night, are difficult to see, but even a glimpse of them is well worth the patience.

If you live, or vacation, along the shores of lakes, rivers, marshes, or the ocean, you have an exclusive variety show to enjoy. If you live in the city, you will find that your parks play host to as many as a dozen species at one time or another.

This book is divided into six chapters: Game Birds, Birds of Prey, Owls, Woodpeckers, Seabirds and Shorebirds, and Songbirds and Others. I have made my selections according to the way in which most guidebooks are arranged, and also according to where I feel certain birds belong. For example, the American magpie does not qualify scientifically as a bird of prey, yet because it was outlawed in Montana in 1927 as a menace to other birds, I feel it should be designated as a bird of prey.

The groups that I have assembled are basically determined as follows: Game Birds include abundant species that are protected for all but a few months of the year when they may be hunted by sportsmen. Birds of Prey include those birds who live upon other birds, their eggs, and their young, as well as fish, snakes, small mammals, and carrion (dead animals). Owls are birds of prey which generally hunt only at night, and Woodpeckers are a unique group of insect-eaters with specialized bills for drilling into wood for their food. Seabirds and Shorebirds include some interesting species that live and hunt for food along the shores, or on the surface, of wetlands, lakes, ponds, streams, and seashores. Songbirds and Others are a variety of interesting birds generally noted for their pleasant voices and bright colors or interesting tricks or traits.

Not all birds could be included in each category, of course. For instance, the varieties of ducks (shorebirds) would fill a library, and so they have been omitted from this introduction to the *Wild Bird World*. I have selected some birds that are common enough to be familiar to you, and some that are uncommon enough to interest you. Read other bird books, watch and listen for birds, and get to know them by song, color, and name. Keep a record of the birds you see and identify. You will be amazed just how fast your list will grow and how your knowledge of the wild bird world about you will grow with it.

Good hunting, good spotting, and good listening; I'm sure you will find much pleasure in all three.

C. B. COLBY

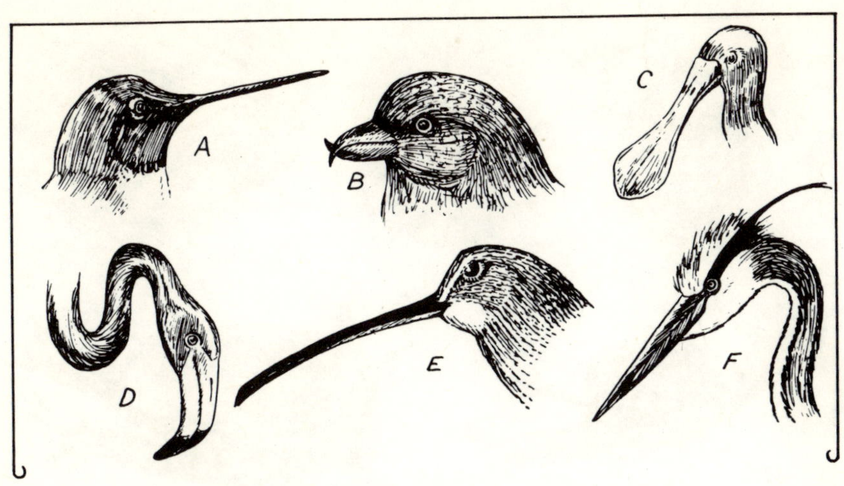

Bills and Beaks

Even if you could not see the birds that own these oddly shaped bills and beaks, you could probably guess what kind of diet each prefers. "A" is the slender bill of a hummingbird, designed to probe for nectar deep in flowers. "B" is the strangely crossed bill of the crossbill, adapted to opening pine cones to reach the seeds inside, upon which this bird depends. The spoonlike bill at "C" belongs to the roseate spoonbill, and is used to sift the sand and silt on marsh bottoms for tiny bits of food. The backward curved bill at "D" is the property of the flamingo, which moves it about the bottom of a pond or marsh to pick up food. At "E" is the long bill of a curlew designed to probe the holes of fiddler crabs and crayfish. "F" shows the "fish spear" bill of the great blue heron, a champion fisher.

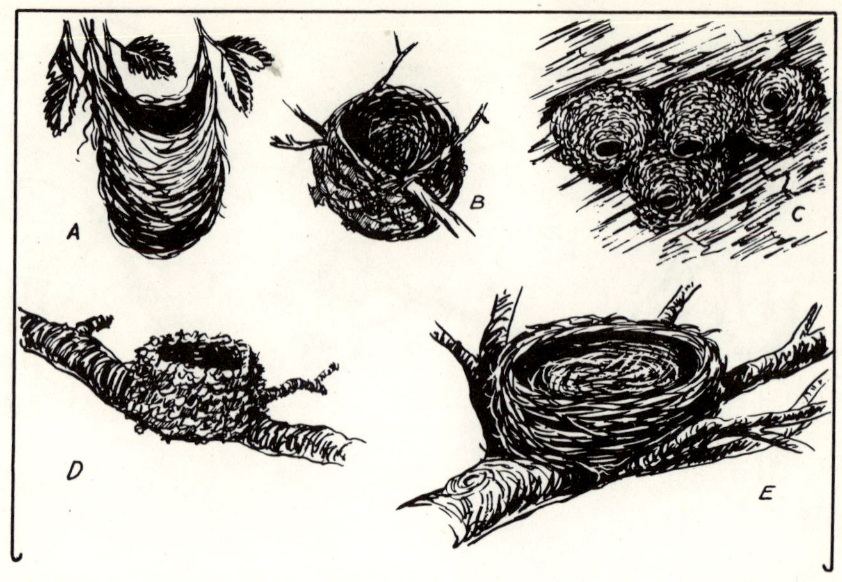

Birds' Nests

A once-popular boys' hobby used to be collecting birds' nests. Now there are more interesting things to collect, and that is just as well, for often the young collectors did not wait until the nests were vacated. Also, many nests are alive with bird lice, nits, and other unpleasant parasites. Take photos of nests or sketch them, but better leave them where they are for another tenant. "A" is the hanging nest of the oriole; "B" shows the nest of many types of warblers and sparrows; and "C" is the clay pellet nest made from wet clay carried in cliff swallows' beaks. The tiny nest at "D" belongs to the hummingbird, and the one at "E" is the mud-lined nest of the robin.

6

Game Birds

CANADA GOOSE

It is a special thrill to hear the honking of a long V-formation of Canada geese as they migrate north in spring or head south in the fall. The Canada goose weighs as much as 14 pounds and measures up to 40 inches in length. It builds huge nests of grasses and of down taken from its body. The gander protects the female goose as she sits on the eggs until they hatch. The young goslings may number up to 7 or 8, and can swim soon after hatching. The youngsters are bright yellow and downy, but they soon take on the color of the adults. The distinctive trademark of all adult Canada geese is the white chin strap. The head, neck, legs, and feet are jet black, as are the wing and tail-tip feathers. When these birds walk, they "toe in" as shown by the tracks at the right. They will return to the same nesting area year after year as long as they are not molested. Adult pairs without youngsters will often kidnap goslings from another pair, and then will fight furiously to keep their new "family."

MOURNING DOVE

At 1 P.M., on September 14, 1914, the last of the species sketched at "A" died. The passenger pigeon had passed into total extinction. This bird was over 20 inches long and had an all-bluish head with red eyes and bluish shoulders. Sketched at the right is the familiar mourning dove, still mistaken for the passenger pigeon by many excited young bird watchers. The mourning dove is about a foot long, a little over half the size of its extinct relative, and has an olive-green head with a pale bluish cap. The eye of the mourning dove is black with a green ring about it. In flight the tail is tipped with white. Note also the identifying black spot just behind and below the eyes of the dove. The "cooooing" of this game bird is heard in almost every state.

RING-NECKED PHEASANT

Originally introduced into the United States from Asia many years ago, the ring-necked pheasant is now common in almost all of the northern states. The cock, which measures as much as a yard long, has a bright green head with a crest, red eye patches, and a white ring about its neck above the shoulders. The rest of the body is brown, white, and black, with flashes of green on the lower back and a ruddy breast. The female is smaller than the male, and her coloring is a mottled brown and black for concealment. When startled this bird rises straight up with a loud whir and then glides away into thick cover. It is a favorite game bird of hunters. Its cry is a loud "cock-cock," often accompanied with a beating of its strong wings. Ring-necked pheasants eat grain, insects, and berries, and may live as long as eight years. In winter they often gather in flocks of a dozen or more to hunt for food.

RUFFED GROUSE

This bird is also known as a partridge and is one of the most popular game birds in the northern United States. The male has a splendid set of black "ruffs" on its shoulders and a black-bordered tail. The general color is brown, white, and black, heavily mottled so that these birds are almost impossible to see until they burst into flight with a muffled roar that frightens many an observer. The ruffed grouse drums the air with its wings, but generally only during the spring mating season. The male averages about 17 inches in length; the female is a bit smaller. They live on seeds, nuts, and berries. They roost in trees and under the snow in winter. "B" shows the foot of a ruffed grouse in summer, and "C" shows it in winter, with little feathery growths added to aid walking in soft snow. Note the short steps they take, shown at "A." For some unknown reason, every fall these birds seem to go "crazy," often killing themselves by flying into cars, buildings, and even people.

SPRUCE GROUSE

This is a truly strange bird. It refuses to be afraid of man. Because of that, it has almost been exterminated in the United States, although it is still plentiful in Canada and in some of the more heavily timbered northern states. The spruce grouse will sit calmly on a branch while a man walks up and grabs it. Often a whole flock, one after another, is captured this way. The spruce grouse is about 15 inches long, with a black tail edged in orange, and its throat and breast have a black area edged in white. There is a bright red rim of naked skin over each eye. The feathered legs are brown. The female is mostly gray, brown, and white in a mottled pattern. Like the ruffed grouse, the spruce grouse often drums with its wings, and sometimes even stops in full flight to hover like a helicopter and drum in the air, looking much like a big fat hummingbird.

WILD TURKEY

Once almost rare, this genuine American game bird is now so plentiful that it is lawful to hunt it in several states. The wild turkey almost became our national bird instead of the bald eagle. Benjamin Franklin was its biggest champion, and he nearly succeeded in having it chosen in place of the eagle because it was huge (up to 20 pounds for an old gobbler); because it had contributed much to the survival of our early settlers; and because it looked so impressive when it strutted about with its big fantail spread. The males have an odd hairlike beard growing from the center of the breast. The females make a crude nest under a bush and lay up to 15 brown and lilac spotted eggs. As soon as the youngsters can fly they all roost in trees when sleeping. They seldom fly except to escape a natural enemy, but are strong fliers when they have to be, unlike the fat and lazy domestic turkey. Their length is about 4 feet, and their colors are reddish brown, bronze, and black.

WOODCOCK

This stubby, long-billed bird is also know as the "timberdoodle."
It lives in thick woodlands and is a prime game bird. Its plumage
is a mottled gray, brown, and white, an almost perfect camouflage
when the bird is on the ground in the woods, where it searches for
earthworms in the ground. The eyes are big and black and set high
on the head. The woodcock can be found from Nova Scotia west
to the Great Lakes, and it winters as far south as Louisiana. During
the mating season the male puts on a spectacular aerial dance, with
spirals and dives that must make its head spin. Its beak is skin-
covered and full of worm-detecting nerves, so as soon as the ground
becomes frozen and too hard to drill it must head south or starve.
Woodcocks are most apt to be seen flying at dusk.

Birds of Prey

AMERICAN MAGPIE

If there was ever a bird version of a "delinquent," the colorful American magpie would win the dubious title. It is hated by most westerners, in its range from Alaska to New Mexico. About 20 inches long, it has an iridescent black head, chest, and back. Its shoulders are black and its wings are dark gray and blue, while its long tail is greenish with blue tips. The eyes and bill are black. So, say its detractors, is its heart, for the American magpie lives by killing young birds of all species, eating unhatched eggs, and even attacking and killing a sickly cow or sheep, or their newborn. It also attacks newly sheared sheep and freshly branded cattle. Besides that diet, it eats insects, carrion, and rodents. Magpies are continually chattering, and they can chuckle, whistle, and imitate other birds or even the human voice. They are still numerous, in spite of many drives to get rid of them.

BALD EAGLE

This huge bird with the snow-white head and tail is our national bird and on our national emblem. To shoot one is a Federal offense. Bald eagles are nearly a yard long and have a 7-foot wingspan. They live on fish, small animals, and some birds, especially waterfowl, so they build their nests close to water. Eagles' nests — called eyries — are often huge and amazingly strong. At the left is shown the most famous eagle's nest of all. It was built in 1890 in Ohio and was used by many generations of eagles, each adding more material to the nest. When it crashed to the ground in 1925, it was over 12 feet high, measured over 8 feet wide at the top, and weighed nearly 2 tons. Bald eagles have yellow beaks, legs, and feet, and very powerful talons. Young eagles do not have the white head and tail, and are occasionally shot for hawks. Hawks are also beneficial, so it is safer not to shoot anything that looks like either one.

20

BELTED KINGFISHER

This bird is probably known to every boy who has ever fished a rural stream. The belted kingfisher lives along stream banks in an underground burrow tunneled as much as 15 feet into a vertical clay bank. It measures about a foot long and is generally slate-blue and white, with a large head topped by a tall "hairy" crest. In this case, the female is more colorful than the male, with a band of chestnut across the lower chest and down the sides. They prefer to eat small fish, but will also dine on frogs, lizards, crayfish, and large insects. They dive for fish from a high perch or from a hovering flight over the water. Their cry is a harsh rattling sound. A smaller relative, the Texas kingfisher, has a greenish color, and in this species the male wears the chestnut band across the chest. In both species, the heavy black bill is used for fishing and for defense of the nest.

CALIFORNIA CONDOR

It is tragic when any species of wildlife is threatened with extinction, and it is doubly tragic when a species is known to be on its way out, and nothing can be done about it. Such is the case of the fabulous California condor. Less than 50 of these giant birds are known to be alive today, far too few to regain a safe number. The condor has a wingspread of nearly 10 feet, and it nests in the almost inaccessible mountain areas of southern California. It is generally a sooty black with underwing feathers of pure white. Only the head is brightly colored: "1" is bluish gray, the "2" areas are yellow-orange, "3" is black, and "5" is bright pink. The bill, "4," is dark brown. The feet are a rich ivory color. These vanishing birds like to sun themselves with wings outspread as shown. They live on carrion and weigh up to 25 pounds. They mate every two years and lay a single egg.

CROW

The common crow is a really entertaining character, a highly intelligent, resourceful, and durable bird. In spite of all the hunters constantly after it, the crow is still on the increase, and its "cawing" can be heard even close to cities, especially when it spots a cat, owl, or raccoon. The crow is about 18 inches long and jet-black from one end to the other. "A" in the sketch shows crow "pellets" — undigested bits of bone, hair, or similar material that are formed into a neat pellet and regurgitated after a meal. "B" shows the crow's track on landing and hopping; "C" shows its swaggering walk with the toe drag behind it. Crows will eat almost anything, from carrion to choice garden foods. They eat seeds, insects, fruit, eggs, and even young birds of other species. They have very keen eyesight and can spot a hunter over long distances, but can be "called" within gun range by experts.

FALCON

These fast-flying birds of prey have been used for many centuries in the sport of falconry. Trained falcons, launched from a wrist or hand, can seek out and bring down small game. These birds are from 10 to 24 inches long, depending upon the species. They have large heads, pointed wings, and narrow, round-ended tails rather than flared tails like hawks or eagles. They are generally light in color with grays and light buffs predominating. Some have a black "moustache" around the neck. Their talons are long, curved, and needle-sharp. They live on birds and small animals, either chasing them in the air or "stooping" (diving) upon them from above at lightning speeds. They are our fastest flying hawks and can be found wherever there is small game. High buildings are occasionally favorite perches for them. This falcon is also known as the "duck hawk."

OSPREY

The osprey is truly one of the best of all bird fishermen. It not only catches fish close to the surface but will dive beneath the water after a 100-foot dive from above. About 23 inches long, it is a skilled flier. The osprey has a brownish back and wings (upper side) with a mottled throat and wing underside and a barred tail. Occasionally it will eat a water snake or frog, but its main diet is fish. After catching one, the osprey will turn the fish so that its head is facing forward to cut down wind resistance as it is being carried back to the nest. The sketch at upper left shows the unique spike-studded pads of the osprey's feet, designed to grasp and securely hold a slippery fish. Ospreys build huge nests in tall trees along waterways and in our coastal areas, and will chase away crows and other hawks that venture near. They have a shrill whistling call and are very noisy around the nest.

RAVEN

This larger version of the common crow is a most interesting bird, and is quite famous in literature. Edgar Allan Poe wrote of it in his famous poem *The Raven;* Odin, chief god of the Norsemen, was escorted by two raven advisers; Noah sent a raven to look for land after the flood; and Elijah was fed by the ravens. These birds are found in all northern parts of America and abroad. They are huge, with a 4-foot wingspan, and they measure nearly 2 feet long. The head and beak are heavy, and their cry is unmistakable. Unlike the crow, they do not "caw." They have a guttural croak as well as an almost musical gurgling sound. Living in remote areas, they nest in hollow trees, returning to the same nest year after year. They mate for life and both birds raise and protect the young. They live on almost anything, including carrion, crabs, insects, small animals, and fish. They also occasionally attack domestic livestock if it is sick or newborn.

26

ROADRUNNER

Although the roadrunner is a member of the cuckoo family, it is far from a silly bird. Nearly 2 feet long, it is generally a mixture of brown, black, and white with light gray legs. Just back of the yellow eye is a light blue patch, and behind this is a bright red patch. The tips of the outer tail feathers are white and the crest has some purple-black tips. This western bird can outrun a stagecoach, and it had rather escape by running than flying, which it only does as a last resort. It lives on lizards, large insects, and even rattlesnakes and an occasional young bird. Its track is unique in that it is like an "X" with two toes facing forward and two facing backward. The roadrunner's call consists of clucking and cooing, and a sound like a whining puppy. The female builds a nest in low branches, using sticks, soft grasses, feathers, and even snakeskins.

SHRIKE

Although generally classed as a songbird, the gray, black, and white shrike is really a bird of prey, for it feeds upon insects, small animals, and birds. The loggerhead shrike is about 10 inches long and is found over most of the United States in one form or another. These birds slightly resemble the mockingbirds of the southern states in coloring, and all species have the black eye patch. They have an unpleasant but efficient habit of impaling their small victims on thorns or barbed-wire fences while dining. The beak of the shrike is sharply hooked for tearing flesh, although the talons are not curved for grasping food like those of other birds of prey. Shrikes can imitate other birds, and their noises are somewhat reminderful of a catbird. Another identification is their peculiar "bounding" flight unique to this species. Because of their dining habits, they are also called "butcher birds."

SWALLOW-TAILED KITE

This is considered the most graceful of all birds. It lives almost entirely in the air, even taking its food aloft and eating as it flies. The kite holds the food in its talons and bends down quickly to tear off a portion with its beak while soaring on outstretched wings. The bird is white except for the outer-wing feather tips and long, distinctively forked tail. Kites are about 2 feet long and have short but stout bluish green feet and legs. They are found in both North and South America, and live on snakes, grasshoppers, lizards, frogs, grubs, and beetles. Rarely, if ever, do they attack birds or animals. Their cry consists of a high-pitched "kee-wee-wee." In winter they gather in small flocks and head for Mexico and Central America to spend the cold months, returning north again in the spring to begin nest building, often in the same place as the year before.

VULTURE

The unpleasant-looking vulture serves a very valuable purpose as the "clean-up" squad for Mother Nature. As such it is protected by law practically everywhere. Vultures clean up dead animals and birds from highways, pastures, and prairies with great efficiency. The black vulture measures up to 27 inches long with a 5-foot wingspread. It is all black with yellowish legs. The larger turkey vulture has a red naked head and pinkish feet and legs. It grows up to 32 inches long and has a 6-foot wingspread. Both species are marvelous soarers and have phenomenal eyesight and sense of smell. They are found in all but the most northern states, but are seldom found over unbroken forests as they need to soar upon the hot air rising from open fields. Usually they are found in flocks, and both species sit with their shoulders hunched and head held low.

Owls

BARN OWL

These birds with the heart-shaped faces are the ones that scare the wits out of someone who climbs into old barns. They are also called "monkey-faced" owls because of the shape of their faces and the dark areas about the eyes. They are about 17 inches long and sit tall instead of crouching down as do most owls. They are found over the eastern and southern parts of the United States, and live almost exclusively on mice, which they hunt for at night. They, like the crows, disgorge "pellets" of undigested food, which can be found under their nesting trees. They also eat large insects, particularly crickets and grasshoppers, and occasionally dine on frogs, rats, and even small birds. They can scream horribly, and hiss, and click their beaks rapidly. Note the odd "comb" under the middle toe, and how they can turn one toe back to make an X-shaped track. They nest in trees, caves, buildings, and ground burrows.

GREAT GRAY OWL

A rare Arctic owl is the great gray owl, North America's largest. It measures up to 30 inches long and hunts in the daylight as well as the dark, although it prefers the nighttime. It does not see as well by daylight as does the snowy owl, and it seeks the darkest shadows when not actually hunting. It lives on small animals — mice, rabbits, squirrels, and birds — for although it is larger than the great horned owl, it is far less powerful. The gray owl can also be found in the northern states when Arctic food is hard to find. It is sketched here for comparison with the tiny elf owl of the southwest. The elf is our smallest owl, and measures less than 6 inches long. The elf owl lives in holes in cactus and plays "dead" when caught. It lives on insects and small mice, and hunts only by night.

GREAT HORNED OWL

This is one of the fiercest and most powerful of all birds. It will attack almost anything, even men who have approached too closely to its nest. It eats rabbits, woodchucks, cats, skunks, poultry, mice, porcupines — almost anything not too large for it to attack. The great horned owl may be 2 feet long with a huge wingspread. It flies silently and attacks with fury. Normally, it has a low cry, consisting of soft hoots, but upon occasion it can yelp like a dog or squall like a cat. Its most unforgettable cry is a piercing scream that will truly make your hair stand on end. This owl is found from coast to coast, and in the Arctic it has a close relative that is almost white. The great horned owl is generally mottled brown, gray, and black, but its eyes are surrounded with a reddish orange area edged with black. It builds its nest in old hawk or crow nests, on cliffs, or, in rare instances, directly on the ground.

SNOWY OWL

The expression "blind as an owl" does not include this bird, for it can see as well in the daylight as in the dark — an unfortunate fact for the crow that happens to pester the snowy owl as it sits "sleeping" on a stump, as this Arctic bird of prey enjoys crow meat as well as any other. The snowy owl lives on lemmings, hare, birds, and fish. If such food is scarce it flies south, even as far as Bermuda, to find it. These birds are powerful and tireless fliers, unlike many other owls, and have been spotted a thousand miles out at sea. Over 2 feet in length and generally snowy white, this owl has a few flecks and bars if you look closely. The female is larger than the male and has more visible flecks and bars on top of the head, wings, and flanks. Snowy owls prefer perching on the ground instead of in trees.

36

Woodpeckers

CALIFORNIA WOODPECKER

This bird must be the champion nut-hoarder of all time. It drills little round holes in trees, church steeples, houses, and poles, and neatly fills them with acorns, sometimes thousands of them. Each acorn is fitted into its hole with the soft end out so that it can easily be eaten later on, as shown at "B." "A" shows a typical storage tree. The California woodpecker has a bright red cap, white forehead and cheeks, and a yellow throat patch. Its body is black with a white belly splotched with black. The tail is white with black tail-feather tips. It has a black eye patch with creamy white eyes. About 9 inches long, it can be found from California as far south as Panama. Occasionally, the woodpecker seems to go haywire and fills holes with pebbles instead of nuts. Perhaps it is trying to fool the squirrels.

FLICKER

Here is our only brown-backed woodpecker, also known as the "yellow-hammer," and it certainly sounds like one. About a foot long, this bird is found all over the eastern part of the United States. Its head and the back of its neck are gray, with a red crescent on the nape of the neck. The throat and eye area are tan, with a sort of black "moustache" at the corners of the mouth. The yellow feathers, or shafts, in its wings also give it the name "yellow-shafted flicker." In the west there is a similar flicker known as the red-shafted flicker; it has red wing feathers. Flickers of various species range from coast to coast and from Alaska to the Gulf of Mexico. They live on insects found in trees and on the ground. Their X-shaped tracks are shown at left. The tail-feather tips are stiff and are used as props to hold them steady while they whack away with their beaks, looking for wood.

HAIRY AND DOWNY WOODPECKERS

These two neighborly woodpeckers dressed in red, black, and white are very similar except for size. The little downy woodpecker is about 6 inches long, while the hairy is 10 inches long. The downy is a frequent visitor to windowsill feeding trays. The larger hairy is much more shy and prefers the deeper woodlands. Both live on insects, woodborers, and some vegetable matter. These birds, as well as closely related species, are found in every part of the United States from border to border, and in Canada as well. They are very valuable aids in the control of insects that do damage to trees, and like all woodpeckers they are protected. Males of both species have red patches on their heads and white backs and undersides. The outer tail feathers of the downy are dotted with black, while those of the hairy are plain. Both species build nests in hollow trees.

NUTHATCH

All you need to attract some little nuthatches is a few sunflower seeds or a hunk of suet. They seem to know when either of these items is in the vicinity and will come in a hurry for their share. The white-breasted nuthatch (right) is the larger of the two, measuring about 5 inches or a bit more. The red-breasted nuthatch (left) measures about 4 inches in length. They both eat insects, nuts, and seeds. The white-breasted bird has a black cap, blue-gray back and wings, and traces of buff on its flanks. The red-breasted nuthatch has a red-orange underside, white cheeks, and a black eye stripe with a narrow white stripe above the eye. The outer tail feathers and wing feathers have white areas. The name "nuthatch" comes from its habit of opening hard-shelled seeds and nuts to get at the insides.

PILEATED WOODPECKER

Other than the very rare ivory-billed woodpecker, this is our largest, measuring nearly 18 inches long. It is one of the bird world's greatest woodchoppers, and has actually toppled trees as much as a foot in diameter, cutting them almost through in several places, looking for ants' nests. It also eats grubs, wood-boring beetles, termites, fruit, and nuts. These brilliantly marked birds have a bright red crest, and the rest of their bodies are startlingly black and white. They build their nests in old trees and excavate the interior to a depth of as much as 3 feet. They can rip out great pieces of wood with their powerful bills; some bills are as big as a man's hand. Their call is similar to that of the flicker, a single note repeated over and over with a rising and falling inflection. They range from Nova Scotia to Texas in several very similar forms.

RED-HEADED WOODPECKER

This bird is the only eastern woodpecker with a completely red head. It averages about 10 inches long; the back, wings, and tail are bluish black and the rump, belly, and rear edge of the wings are white. It lives on fruit, nuts, and millions of insects. Unlike the rest of the woodpeckers, it is fond of grasshoppers and flies. Usually, it will nest in tall stumps or dead trees, but if none are available it will also nest in telephone poles, fence posts, and holes in buildings. The young of the species do not have a red head until the spring after they are born. Until then they wear a brown outfit all over, and have often been mistaken for another species. These woodpeckers, like the flicker and Lewis woodpecker of the west, are the only species that regularly feed upon the ground.

WHITE-HEADED AND LEWIS WOODPECKERS

One of the things that reveals the great size of the United States is the fact that wildlife that is familiar to one area may never be seen in the opposite end of the country. Here, for example, are two woodpeckers common to the western regions of America, but unknown in the east. At the left is the 9-inch white-headed woodpecker, living on the west coast, and at the right is the gray-bibbed Lewis woodpecker, a couple of inches longer. It is found from Canada to New Mexico, and was discovered by Lewis and Clark in 1804-06. The bird at the left has a white head with a red patch on the back, and white outer-wing feathers. The rest of it is black. The Lewis woodpecker has a red belly and face area and a white band across the back of the head. The rest of its body is brownish black. Instead of drilling, this bird catches insects on the ground and on bark and leaves. The white-headed woodpecker uses his short bill like a crowbar, prying bark from trees for the insects beneath. It particularly likes pine seeds.

Seabirds and Shorebirds

BOOBY BIRD

The booby's name comes from the Spanish word *bobo*, meaning a dunce, or stupid one, and the name certainly is suitable. The snapshot from which this sketch was made was taken on Mona Island in the Caribbean. After taking the picture, the photographer walked up and pushed the bird off the branch with his hand. You can even push them off their nests and look at their eggs, and they will just sit and stare stupidly at you until you leave. All four of their toes are connected with webs, and their feet and legs are bright red. The heads are a pale yellow, the bodies are white, and the wing feathers are tipped in black. These red-footed boobies nest in trees, while their relatives, the white-bellied boobies (dark gray, yellow feet and legs, and a white underside), nest on ledges or flat ground. They measure nearly 30 inches long and are expert fliers, swimmers, and divers. They live on fish and other marine life that they catch near their nests.

GREAT BLUE HERON

It seems impossible that a bird as big as this (over 40 inches long with a wingspread of over 6 feet) can be as invisible as it sometimes seems. It stands motionless along a marsh edge or a stream. ready to spear or grab its food as it comes near. The heron lives on frogs, fish, snakes, grasshoppers, rats, mice, young muskrats, lizards, and even other birds. Sometimes herons live in colonies, but they usually live alone or with a mate. The nest may be as high as 40 feet above the water and as wide as a yard across. They are found almost from coast to coast. In winter they usually move south, but they can stand cold weather if the fishing is good. One interesting fact about this huge heron is the unique comb (shown at "A") built under its center toe. This is called a pecten and is thought to be used to remove tiny bird lice from the heron's feathers.

50

KILLDEER

This member of the plover family can be heard calling "kill-dee" over almost all of the United States from New England to California, and from Hudson Bay to Florida. A brown-backed bird with an orange-brown rump and tail and twin chest bars of black, it nests on the ground in open fields. It bobs its head as it walks, and toes in, making the odd track that is sketched at the right. The killdeer is about 10 inches long and lives on insects, earthworms, and small marine life. It likes to live near some sort of water, where it can hunt for food. It can run very fast and is a swift flier, often active at night and especially on moonlight nights. If its nest is approached it will fly around the intruder's head, screaming loudly and darting to drive him away. Its call consists of many whistles as well as its trademark call of "kill-dee kill-dee, kill-dee!" It has also taken to such man-made areas as lawns and golf courses.

LOON

If you have ever heard anyone call another person "crazy as a loon," this is the bird he was referring to. However, the loon is anything but crazy. The only odd thing about this big (32 inches) waterfowl is its cry, which sounds like wild laughter. The loon is black and white barred, with a black head and throat bar, or bib. In winter it is gray above and white below. An expert diver, the loon can swim long distances underwater. It lives almost exclusively on fish, and builds its nest close to the water, if possible on a small island. It is never more than a few feet from the water, as it can only crawl on land or flop along with great effort. The young can get about on land better than the parents, in little hops and jumps. The loon is found in the northern states and Canada, where it prefers quiet lakes.

MAN-O'-WAR BIRD

The poet Walt Whitman said of this fabulous flier, "Thou art all wings." He was nearly correct, for this bird, weighing between 3 and 4 pounds, has a 7-foot wingspan. Almost a quarter of its total weight is made up of its shoulder girdle and breast muscles, which power its fantastically long wings. It can fly almost effortlessly for hours. It lives on fish picked from the surface of the water, and it never gets a feather wet. The man-o'-war also pursues other water birds, and makes them drop their catches, which it then snatches as the food falls through the air. The male has a huge inflatable bright red throat-sac, which it expands to enormous size during the breeding season to attract a mate. The man-o'-war bird is an iridescent blue-black. The young have a white underside and a yellowish head until they mature. There are several related species of the man-o'-war bird found on islands about the oceans of the world.

SEA GULL

This is the gull most familiar to people who live along beaches. The adult has a slate-blue back and black barred wing tips, with the rest of the body white. The heavy beak is yellow and the legs and feet a pinkish brown. The young gulls are all mottled gray-brown, but they change to adult plumage when fully grown. They are found on both coasts and in Canada as well as inland, wherever there is water and food. They do not insist upon the water being salty, and so are also found about the Great Lakes. All these gulls are scavengers. They live on fish, and such things as clams, which they drop from a height upon rocks and highways (and sometimes people) to open. They are very noisy and gather in huge flocks wherever there is food. About 2 feet long, they are unexcelled soarers. In fact, many aircraft and glider designers have studied the gull's anatomy and skill in soaring.

54

TROPIC BIRD

The Pacific and Indian oceans are home to the graceful and unique tropic bird. There are several species, and all are noted for their unique tail feathers. The one or two central feathers are much longer than the rest, often measuring as long as 18 inches, and have a thin, wiry appearance. Polynesians prize these feathers as decorations, but they do not harm the birds to get them. They deftly pull the feathers from the birds as they sit on their nesting sites. A tropic bird lives on small fish, squid, and similar marine life, which it grabs after diving upon them. The bird runs from 18 inches to a yard in length, and its only call is a harsh croak or chatter, but if molested on its nesting site it will peck, snap its beak, and scream loudly. It does not build a nest, but lays a single egg on a ledge or in a cavity, to keep it from rolling away. Its tiny feet make standing difficult for the tropic bird.

TUFTED PUFFIN

This short chunky bird with the wild hairdo is also known as a "sea parrot." It lives in Alaska and along the Siberian coasts. Fish is its main diet, and it is adept at stealing the bait right off a fisherman's line. About 15 inches long, the puffin's body is mostly a rich chocolate-brown with darker back and wings. Its face is white with yellowish hair plumes on each side. The eye is rimmed in bright red and the outer portions of its peak are also red. The section of beak next to its face is greenish yellow. The legs and webbed feet are bright red and the nails jet-black. In winter the plumes disappear along with the white markings, and it even sheds the bright outer covering of the parrotlike bill. The puffin's nest is made of a few bits of grass and ground rubbish in a shallow burrow or occasionally under a sheltering bush. It lays a single egg.

VIRGINIA RAIL

The familiar expression "thin as a rail" could mean thin as a fence rail, or thin as a Virginia rail, for this marsh bird is a lot thinner than it looks. It can compress its body and feathers so that it can easily slip between marsh grasses an inch or less apart, which seems incredible. The Virginia rail is about 9 inches long, and is reddish brown with a brown and white barred underside and a gray patch on the sides of its head. The underside of the short erect tail is also heavily spotted in brown and white. It lives on aquatic insects and other marine life along the shore. The nest is roofed over with rushes and marsh grass to form a shade and shelter, and it is deeply hollowed and built just above the water. The rail's cry is a "ticket-ticket-ticket" or a "racket-racket-racket" depending upon how it sounds to you. The male and female look alike.

WILSON'S SNIPE

This is our only chunky shorebird with such a long bill and a white barred head. The snipe's general coloring is a mottled brown and white, with a large black eye rimmed in pale yellow. The feet and legs are also a pale yellow. The belly is dirty white with the sides heavily barred with brown. It can be found from Alaska to Newfoundland and as far south as California and Pennsylvania. Unlike the bills of most birds, the bill of the snipe is covered with skin that helps it probe the earth for worms. Delicate sense organs under this skin help to locate the underground worms. The snipe is about 11 inches long, and builds its nest on a grassy tussock, usually surrounded by water as protection. They are popular game birds, but they fly fast and in zigzag courses and are very elusive targets. Note the odd track at the upper left of the illustration.

Songbirds and Others

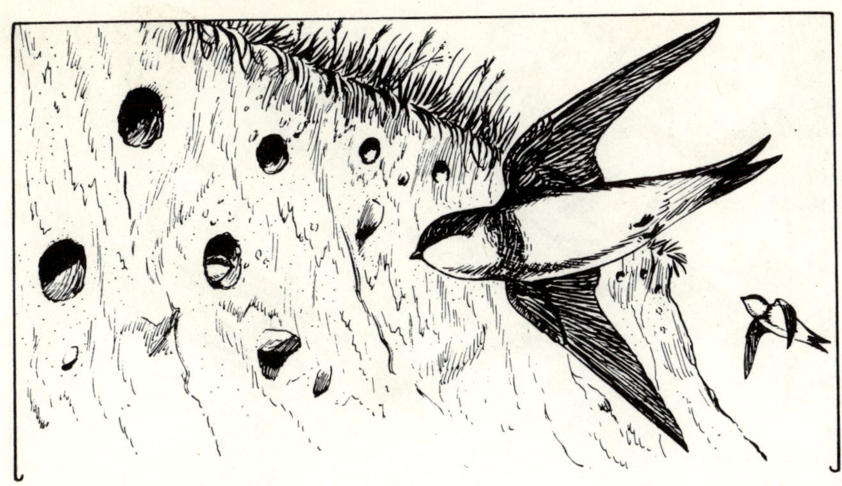

BANK SWALLOW

Dusky gray-brown and white and as nimble as anything that flies, the bank swallow builds its nest in riverbanks. Small boys often lie atop sandbanks and try to catch one with their caps as it zips in and out of its home. They never even come close. Often dozens, or even over a hundred, swallows will tunnel into the same bank and live together in a big colony. They are a little over 5 inches long and live on all sorts of insects, which they catch on the wing. They fly by day and stay in their nests at night when it is too dark to hunt. Their tunnels are dug into the bank for 2 or 3 feet, with the nest at the end, lined with soft grasses. They get along with the noisy kingfisher and often build in the same bank that he does, even using the kingfisher's tunnel to get to their own nests. Their voice is soft and consists of twitters and a sound that can only be spelled as "speedz-sweet, speedz-sweet."

BLUE JAY

This brilliant blue, black, and white eastern blue jay is a fine if noisy neighbor to almost all neighborhoods. It measures about a foot long, and is 12 inches of curiosity, excitement, fiendishness, and flashing color. The blue jay robs birds' nests, chases crows, warns game of approaching hunters, consumes tons of birdseed put out for other birds, and generally has a great deal of fun out of everything going on around it. The blue jay has a blue crested head, and a back and tail decorated with bars of black. Its wings are trimmed in white, and it has a white throat edged with black. The breast is generally a pale yellow, while the bill, feet, and legs are jet-black. Its voice can be loud and excited or soft and gentle. It is a clever imitator of the calls of other birds. The blue jay stores surplus food by burying it, and when on the ground, will hop instead of walk. In spite of its noise and bad habits, you can't help liking it.

CANADA JAY

This is the counterpart of our familiar blue jay. It looks like a king-sized chickadee, with almost the same markings and black and buff coloring except that the Canada jay does not have the black bib of the chickadee. This jay is also known as "whisky jack" and "camp robber." It is a good robber. It will steal food, matches, cigarettes, and anything else small enough to cart away. Generally it lives on more palatable items like insects and small mice. Almost a foot long, it is gray-backed with a black cap and eye patches. The wings are darker gray and the tail feathers are dark with a narrow white tip-line. The Canada jay builds its nests in trees and is frequently found in the most northern states, as well as in Canada. The Oregon jay on the west coast looks very similar and is equally full of curiosity. Its voice includes assorted typical blue jay noises plus a sharp whistle.

CARDINAL

One spot of bright color that can be relied upon to brighten up the dullest winter day is the cardinal. This bright red bird with the black around its bill is a cheerful visitor to almost any feeding tray. Its mate is greenish brown but also has the reddish crest and red bill. Male and female are usually together and make a pleasant flash of color. Cardinals are found over most of the east, and measure about 7 inches long. They are not really migratory, and so are around all year. They live on seeds and often travel in small flocks. The male is a fine mate, often feeding the female as she sits on the nest and then helping with the feeding of the young cardinals after they hatch. They build their nests in a thick bush or tangled vine. As soon as the young are hatched, the male takes over their training while the female starts another nest for a second family in the same year.

CEDAR WAXWING

There are three species of waxwings; the cedar waxwing shown here, the Bohemian waxwing found in the northwest and up into Alaska, and the Japanese waxwing, found in eastern Asia. The cedar waxwing has an olive-green body with a fine tuft or crest, a rosy breast, and a yellow lower belly. Its tail and rump are bluish gray as are its wing feathers, and it has a bright yellow tip to its tail feathers. There is also a bit of red on the tips of some of its wing feathers. Its face and the underside of its chin are black, and a fine line of black runs from the corner of the eye up over the head behind the crest. The Bohemian waxwing is almost identical, but has some yellow and white on its wings. These birds are insect- and berry-eaters. They make poorly constructed nests in bushes or low branches. Some winters they migrate as far south as Panama, but at other times they spend the winter in the southern United States.

CHICKADEE

About the most friendly thing in nature, or at least in the bird world, is the chickadee. This happy-go-lucky creature with the black cap, black bib, and buff-colored sides is the black-capped chickadee. Out west there are chickadees with brown caps, called Hudsonian chickadees; one with a white stripe over the eye, known as the mountain chickadee; and another with a brown back called the chestnut-backed chickadee. They all nest in hollow trees and have similar calls — the cheerful "chickadee-dee-dee-dee." The black-capped neighbor also has a two-note (one high and one low) call in the spring. All chickadees live on insects, larvae, moth eggs, and seeds. They love suet and sunflower seeds, and will come to your hand if you are patient and quiet. They lend a lot of fun and optimism to the dreariest of winter days — all for a few seeds on your windowsill.

COWBIRD

This iridescent blue-black bird with the brown head has a rather sneaky trait. Like some humans, it refuses to assume any responsibility for its offspring, and it lets someone else bring them up and feed them while it goes off to have a good time. These birds, so named for their habit of following cattle in order to feed on the insects stirred up as the cattle walk through the grass, lay their eggs in the nests of other birds rather than in a nest of their own. The young cowbird hatches and grows rapidly, demanding constant feeding and often pushing out or killing the real youngsters of the adopted parents. The female cowbird lays about five eggs, each one in a different nest while the nest owner is away. Then the cowbird goes off to enjoy life without responsibilities. It is about 7 inches long, and lives on spiders, seeds, insects, grain, and berries.

EVENING GROSBEAK

This heavyset, chunky bird is the evening grosbeak, found along our northern borders and occasionally down into New England. A western variety lives as far north as Alberta, Canada. The evening grosbeak seems to prefer the colder portions of North America and up into Canada. It measures 8 inches, and is a colorful bird, with a bright orange-yellow body and yellow forehead. The cap is black and the rest of the head to the shoulders is a light chocolate brown. The tail and wing primary feathers (outer ones) are black, while the inner or secondary wing feathers are white. The bill is short, heavy, and an ivory color. This bird eats all kinds of seeds, from apple to pine, and in summer seems to have a hankering for salt. At the feeding tray, it heads for the sunflower seeds. Although it is a swift flier, the evening grosbeak appears quite sluggish when on the ground and spends a great deal of time just sitting.

GOLDEN-CROWNED KINGLET

These pleasant little birds are even smaller than the peppy chicka-dee. They are 4 inches long, olive-green in color, with a golden-crowned head edged with a border of black and white. The crown of the male has an orange stripe down the center of the golden area, while the female wears a plain golden patch. They are found over most of the United States in winter, to add color to the scenery, but they migrate somewhat south in extreme weather. Kinglets are very tame and sociable, even at times perching on a rake as you work in the yard. Their high-pitched "zee-zee-zee" seems to say that they are glad to see someone working for a change. They live on insects and spiders, and build their tiny nests of green moss and soft grasses, lined with feathers. Their nests are usually found in pine trees or other conifer trees. Kinglets often travel in flocks.

GRACKLE

Two species of grackles may be found over all of the eastern United States. The purple grackle is about 13 inches long, and the larger boat-tailed grackle is about 16 inches long. The larger bird gets its name from the fact that, when flying, the center of its long tail is lower than the sides, and the tail looks like the keel of a boat. Both species prefer to live near water, the boat-tailed often wading in up to its breast. They feed on mollusks, water insects, land insects, grain grubs, seeds, and berries, as well as some eggs and even young birds. Both sexes of the purple grackle are an iridescent bronze-black, and the boat-tailed grackles are a brownish color. Neither species can sing, but they get along pretty well with assorted raucous squeaks and squawks that sound somewhat like a rusty door hinge. Flocks of grackles often number in the thousands, and may be a mile or more in length. They winter in the southern states.

JUNCO

One of the most frequent visitors to a feeding station is this neatly dressed seed-eater, the slate-colored junco. It is about 6 inches long and a warm gray color except for the lower chest, which is pure white. The wings are darker gray as is the tail. The outer tail feathers are white, and they are visible when it flies. The junco lives on seeds, and can be found from Alaska to Nova Scotia, generally wintering from eastern Canada to the Gulf of Mexico. It is also popularly called the "snowbird." In the west there is a larger species with white wing bars. Juncos have reddish eyes, pink bills, and pinkish legs and feet. They have a sort of "fluttering" flight and are popular with winter bird feeders, for they will come readily to windowsill feeding trays for almost any kind of seeds. They often fight among themselves for the "handout" with a great deal of wing flapping and chatter.

LARK

Country dwellers enjoy the sweet musical song of the meadowlark (left), which winters in the south and then returns north in the spring to build its nest in or under the dried grass from last year's crop. Its throat and belly are golden and there is a crescent of black across the chest. Its head is brown and white striped, and the outer tail feathers are white. The bird at the right is the horned lark of the United States and Canada, except for the Gulf area. The horned lark lacks the golden breast of the meadowlark but has a similar black breastband. It has a dirty white front and a brown head decorated with two "horns" of hairlike feathers that can be erected at will — hence the name. The horned lark measures about 7 inches in length, while the more familiar meadowlark is over 10 inches long. They both eat seeds and insects, and are pleasant summer visitors.

NIGHTHAWK

Perhaps you have seen these swiftly darting birds in the evening skies, looking for insects, or screaming down in a bulletlike dive as their wings make a sudden purring sound. They are about 10 inches long, and are not actually hawks at all, but members of the goatsucker family, which also includes the whippoorwill and the chuckwill's-widow. The nighthawk has a plaintive call of "feeeeb" as it flies, and when at rest it is almost impossible to locate. Its coloring is a mottled brown and black. When it sits on a branch it always perches lengthwise rather than across it. It has a white throat patch and a white bar across its tail and outer wing feathers. It feeds upon insects, from tiny gnats to huge moths and dragonflies. As many as several thousand insects have been found in the stomach of one nighthawk.

ORIOLE AND REDSTART

These two birds are often confused because of their similar coloring, although they are obviously quite different when seen together. The smaller redstart (left) is about 5 inches long with orange on its tail, wings, and flanks. Its underside below the back and chest is white. The Baltimore oriole measures over 7 inches in length, and is also black, white, and orange. The orange on the larger bird is on its underside, rump, and outer tail feathers, as well as the shoulders. The orchard oriole of the south-central states is similarly marked, but is chestnut instead of yellow-orange. All of these colorful singers are insect-eaters, but they also love grapes. The Baltimore oriole was named for Lord Baltimore, who founded the city of Baltimore, Maryland. Lord Baltimore's colors were also bright orange and black.

PURPLE FINCH

This bird is not purple, in spite of its name. It is more pink than purple, and only the male has any color at all. The female is as dull as a sparrow and almost impossible to identify. The male is a mixture of brown and white mottles, with a pale pinkish coloration mixed in. The tail is short and brown, and the wing primary feathers are also brown. The short, strong beak is brownish ivory. The finch was originally a wild bird, but it has become so used to man and his buildings that it often nests in yard evergreens where it can sponge free food from a feeding station. It is a quarrelsome bird and will often drive other birds away from the tray. Various species of these misnamed birds are found from coast to coast except in the arid midwestern states. During courtship the male often plays dead until the female pecks it.

RED-EYED TOWHEE

This bird can be easily spotted because of its unique brown, white, and black dress. The head, throat, back, and rump are all black. The breast is white and the flanks are russet brown. The tail is black with white tips, and its eyes are bright red. There are white tips on some of its wing feathers. Its cheery "cheewink" call is also a good identification. The towhee enjoys hunting for food on the ground, and it scatches busily among the leaves for insects. A western species is similar but has white spots on its wings and back. It is found in Canada and the United States eastward to Maine and south to Georgia, wintering as far south as Florida and Texas. The towhee builds its nest on the ground or in brush piles, and it is a skillfully made affair, lined with fine materials and hair. The female is generally all brown in color with a white belly and white outer tail feathers.

REDWING BLACKBIRD

This colorful resident of marshes and wetlands is about 9 inches long, and is jet-black except for the bright red and orange epaulets on its shoulders. The upper portion of the shoulder patches is red, and the lower rim is a bright orange or yellow. The blackbird's call is a musical "okkk-a-leeeee," ending on a high note. It also has a high-pitched alarm note and a short cackle. The female is mostly brown, white, and gray, with a slight suggestion of a reddish shoulder patch. They build their nests in bulrushes and tall grasses, anchoring them to the growing blades. Sometimes one side grows faster than the other and tips the eggs into the water. They eat weed seeds, weevils, and a great number of insects. Redwing blackbirds range from the Atlantic to the Pacific, varying slightly in wing and bill proportions among the closely related species.

ROBIN

It would not be spring without the first robin to make it official. This member of the thrush family is usually the first summer bird to appear on lawns, often while snow is still in the air. It measures about 10 inches in length, has a black head, an orange-red breast, a striped throat, and small white spots over the eye. Its call of "cheerily, cheerily, cheerily" is often heard before rain, and its excited cry of alarm when a cat is in the area is unmistakable and familiar. Robins have many natural enemies — cats, snakes, jays, owls, hawks, and crows — but in spite of them they build their homes over most of Canada and the United States. Their nests are sturdy affairs of twigs, grass, and mud, lined with soft materials. They build them in trees and among the rafters of all sorts of buildings. Their youngsters are chubby copies of the parents, with short tails and large brown spots on their breasts.

RUBY-THROATED HUMMINGBIRD

This 3-inch bird can fly in all directions, even backward, almost faster than the eye can follow. In spite of its size, it can fly across the 500-mile-wide Gulf of Mexico without trouble. It is an iridescent green with a flashing crimson throat above a white breast area. The female is similar, but without the ruby throat. Hummingbirds have a variety of calls, including shrill squeals, chirps, and twitterings. They live on insects and nectar, which they dip from flowers with long slender bills and fine extensible tongues. They are pugnacious and will defend their nests against an enemy. The nests, hardly larger than a thimble, are placed on a horizontal branch and lined with plant down and covered with soft lichens. Hummingbirds can be attracted to a yard or garden with little bottles full of sugar and water. The wings of these tiny "helicopters" beat from 50 to 75 times a second.

SCARLET TANAGER

One of the bird world's "flashiest dressers," with a bright red body and head and jet-black wings and tail, the scarlet tanager adds color to the landscape wherever it is. The male is a little over 7 inches long. It has a yellowish green mate, often mistaken for another species. In the south and west there is a summer tanager, which resembles the scarlet tanager but has reddish black wings and tail. The female is also colored yellowish green. They build their nests comparatively low, but out of reach of humans, and they seem to prefer oaks and hemlocks for their nesting. They spend winters in Colombia or Bolivia, leaving the United States in October. They feed on seeds and berries but their main diet is insects of all kinds. Some springs they come north too soon, before the caterpillars upon which they expect to feed are hatched, and then thousands of tanagers starve.

SWIFT

These birds, often seen darting around the evening skies, are close relatives of the hummingbirds. They spend most of their daylight hours in seemingly tireless flight. Like swallows, their legs and feet are tiny and almost useless on the ground. In the air swifts are the fastest of birds, sometimes attaining speeds of over 200 miles an hour. They live entirely on insects, caught on the wing, and they range from one corner of the globe to the other. They build their nests of bark, twigs, and similar materials held together with their gluey saliva. Here are four species of swifts: "A," the black swift, 7 inches long; "B," the white-throated swift, 6 inches long; "C," the white-rumped swift; and "D," the little 4-inch Vaux swift. All are gray, black, or white in various combinations, with tiny pinkish feet. They build their nests in chimneys or cliffs.

WHIPPOORWILL AND CHUCK-WILL'S-WIDOW

The whippoorwill (left) and chuck-will's-widow (right), like the nighthawk, live entirely on insects, or "meat." In fact, the widow has been known to eat warblers, sparrows, and hummingbirds. They are both mottled brown, white, and black with few distinctive markings. The whippoorwill has a faint white throat-bib. The male has white outer tail feathers and those of the female are buff. The widow also has a faint light throat band. Both have huge mouths from side to side, but small bills. Stiff bristles about the mouth help snare insects that the bird catches after dark and on the wing. They perch lengthwise on branches or the ground. Their calls identify them — an oft-repeated "whip-poor-will" and "chuck-will's-widow." "Will" is accented by the first, and the "wid" of "widow" by the latter.

Bird Facts at a Glance

Game Birds	Size of Male (Female usually smaller)	Predominant Colors	Found in U.S.
Canada Goose	to 40 in.	black, gray, white	generally northern and eastern areas
Mourning Dove	12 in.	green, black, pale blue, white tail feather tips in flight	throughout U.S.
Ring-necked Pheasant	to 36 in.	brown, white, black, green	northern U.S.
Ruffed Grouse	17 in.	brown, mottled white, black	northern U.S.
Spruce Grouse	15 in.	black, brown, white	few northern states
Wild Turkey	48 in.	reddish brown, bronze, black	some areas in eastern U.S.
Woodcock	11 in.	gray, brown, white	Great Lakes to east coast
Birds of Prey			
American Magpie	20 in.	black, blue, white	western U.S.
Bald Eagle	36 in.	dark brown, white	throughout U.S.
Belted Kingfisher	12 in.	blue, white, chestnut	throughout U.S.
California Condor	10-ft. wingspread	gray, orange, black, brown	California, nearly extinct
Crow	18 in.	black	throughout U.S.
Falcon	to 24 in.	gray, buff, brown	throughout U.S. in one or another species
Osprey	23 in.	brown, white, gray	throughout U.S.
Raven	24 in.	black	remote areas
Roadrunner	24 in.	brown, black, white	western U.S.
Shrike	10 in.	gray, black, white	throughout U.S.
Swallow-tailed Kite	24 in.	white, black	throughout U.S.
Vulture	27 in.	black	throughout U.S., except most northern states
Owls			
Barn Owl	17 in.	gray, brown, white	eastern, southern U.S.
Great Gray Owl	to 30 in.	gray	northern U.S.

Owls	Size of Male (Female usually smaller)	Predominant Colors	Found in U.S.
Great Horned Owl	to 24 in.	brown, gray, black	throughout U.S.
Snowy Owl	24 in.	white	Arctic regions

Woodpeckers			
California Woodpecker	9½ in.	black, white, red	California
Downy Woodpecker	6 in.	red, white, black	throughout U.S.
Flicker	12 in.	brown, gray, yellow	eastern U.S.
Hairy Woodpecker	10 in.	red, white, black	throughout U.S.
Lewis Woodpecker	11 in.	red, white, black	throughout U.S.
Nuthatch			
Red-breasted	4 in.	tan, white, black	throughout U.S.
White-breasted	5 in.	black, blue-gray, white	throughout U.S.
Pileated Woodpecker	18 in.	red, black, white	throughout U.S.
Red-headed Woodpecker	10 in.	red, black, white	eastern U.S.
White-headed Woodpecker	9 in.	white, black	western U.S.

Seabirds and Shorebirds			
Booby Bird	30 in.	yellow, white, black	usually not found in U.S.
Great Blue Heron	40 in.	blue, gray, black	throughout U.S.
Killdeer	10 in.	brown, orange, black	throughout U.S.
Loon	32 in.	black, white	northern U.S.
Man-o'-war Bird	40 in.	blue-black	off U.S. coasts
Sea Gull	24 in.	blue, black, white	coastal areas
Tropic Bird	18 in.	black, white	Pacific Ocean
Tufted Puffin	15 in.	brown, white	Alaska
Virginia Rail	9 in.	reddish brown, white	interior marshlands
Wilson's Snipe	11 in.	brown, white	California, northern U.S.

Songbirds and Others			
Bank Swallow	5 in.	gray-brown, white	throughout U.S., except central interior

Songbirds and Others	Size of Male (Female usually smaller)	Predominant Colors	Found in U.S.
Blue Jay	12 in.	blue, black, white	eastern U.S.
Canada Jay	12 in.	gray, black	northern U.S.
Cardinal	7 in.	red, black	eastern U.S.
Cedar Waxwing	7 in.	gray, green, yellow	southern U.S.
Chickadee	4¾ in.	black, buff	throughout U.S.
Chuck-will's-widow	12½ in.	brown, white, black	throughout U.S.
Cowbird	7 in.	blue-black	throughout U.S.
Evening Grosbeak	8 in.	orange-yellow	northern borders
Golden-crowned Kinglet	4 in.	olive-green, yellow	throughout U.S.
Grackle			
Boat-tailed	16 in.	brown	southern U.S.
Purple	13 in.	bronze-black	southern U.S.
Junco	6 in.	gray, white	Alaska, eastern U.S.
Lark			
Horned	7 in.	brown, white	throughout U.S.
Meadowlark	10 in.	golden, black	throughout U.S.
Nighthawk	10 in.	brown, black, white	throughout U.S.
Oriole	7 in.	black, white, orange	throughout U.S.
Purple Finch	5¾ in.	brown, white, pink	throughout U.S.
Red-eyed Towhee	8 in.	brown, white, black	eastern U.S.
Redstart	5 in.	white, orange	throughout U.S.
Redwing Blackbird	9 in.	black, red	throughout U.S.
Robin	10 in.	black, red	throughout U.S.
Ruby-throated Hummingbird	3 in.	white, red, green	throughout U.S.
Scarlet Tanager	7 in.	red, black	throughout U.S.
Swift	7 in.	black, white, gray	throughout U.S.
Whippoorwill	10 in.	brown, white, black	throughout U.S.

Index